Immortal Realizations

Edward L. Hannon

Content

Edward L. Hannon©

Foreword

This book serves as a flagship for the immortal journey that one has or will take within "THE SELF."

Acknowledgement

I would like to thank "SOURCE CONSCIOUNESS" for gifting me the ability to write these collective works; which will be the existential syllabus for tomorrow's potentiality. I would also like to greatly thank all those who contributed to Microsoft Clipart; which helped greatly to illustrate some of the concepts mentioned in this book.

Philosychology

Philosychology (noun) is a study of conscious behavior created by PhTCB (philosopher and teacher of conscious behavior) Edward L. Hannon. This science is a synthesis of empirical psychology along with his philosophies to methodize a practical or practicable solution to resolve the dilemmas, conflicts, or queries that mankind perpetuates upon itself.

Chaplain Edward Lewis Hannon D.D. (Doctor of Divinity)

I never feel bereft by others' psychologically insecure antics; for, I ultimately know that they are trying to cushion themselves from the misfortune of their own self-defeating potential.

Please remember that irresponsible weapon enthusiasm can be subtly attached to the restrictive experience of unnecessary psychological and physical captivity.

If you have given someone prudent advice, do not allow yourself to become burdened by the egotistical stress of whether or not it is heeded.

When offering sound advice, try not to speak too long; thereby, you will not find yourself vexed, disappointed or insulted by the short attention span of those who are psychologically committed to remain utterly reckless.

Do not undermine or squander the value of what you could exclusively offer; on those, who are habitually apt to discount your personal sense of kindness.

Weak minds typically have an insecure thirst for control; thereby, they will always find themselves stifled by those who could care less about their fragile ambitions for dominance.

There are many who would endeavor to try to ruin your reputation; but, do not give them the leeway of leverage, by egotistically allowing your sense of self-esteem to become utterly vulnerable.

Never reverence a convention, social structure or religion that does not have the common sense to realize that its existential survival is ultimately contingent upon respect; which it should be willing to humbly reciprocate unto others.

Through utter transparency, the prudent voice of truth's liberties can be heard rather soundly.

On the path of solitude, one can find love; through the faithful devotion of personal honesty.

To those that have a hatred for the LBGTQ+ community, but profess to be of a loving religion that is ordained by GOD, remember that primarily the traditional union of heterosexual biological behavior, tendencies, preferences and cells are solely capable of birthing or producing the profound effects of alternative potentialities. So, as it has been Biblically written: "Beloved let us love one another…"

Do not feel that you need a soulmate or a twin flame to validate your existence; for, if you do, you may find that your self-fulfilling potential is helplessly anchored in an incomplete state of psychological distraction.

Once you strive to be just, you may find yourself labeled a villain; by those who have grown accustomed to polarizing their existential perspective.

Never feel intimidated by anyone whose sense of boldness is vainly enabled by an organization with a limited essence of personal identity.

If you carry a profound sense of hatred that would cause you to jeopardize your personal well-being, and face possible incarceration, then you may be a damn derelict; who is an emotional captive of your own illogical outlook.

I find that it is quite impractical to grieve for the demise of defiant hearts; especially, knowing that they did not care enough for themselves to prudently invest in personal transformation.

If no one is listening, then it is a prudent opportunity to withdraw; and give complete audience to that inner voice.

Dear LBGTQ+ community, if you want to be taken seriously do not dress up in apparel that would offend those who you are protesting against; instead, dress in appropriate attire, in order to remind them of the dismal reality from whence you came.

Those who can see tomorrow inherently understand that any moment can become its ancestor of possibilities.

Life has taught me to be patiently still; and leave the hustle and bustle of competitiveness to those who anxiously feel that they are running out of time.

Some of the best masterpieces are produced by those who are an ever pupil of their creative impulses.

Negativity is essential, even within a positive mentality; for, it can keep us prudently mindful of how to alchemically turn a base situation into a golden opportunity.

Appreciate those who are willfully foolish; for they can teach you the personal discernment of how to not waste your time on those that firmly revel in folly.

Stupidity is typically known to mask itself in arrogance.

DIVINITY, in human form, gazes at the vastness of the ocean; as a vital reminder: that although ITS magnitude is ubiquitously exceeding, humility must never be forgotten.

Never undervalue your personal perspective on a matter; simply because someone introduces themselves by a particular title.

Once you have total confidence in yourself, do not expect much external support; especially, if you are dealing with those who primarily find a sense of strength, validation or purpose by identifying with the dynamics of a group.

$$\Sigma$$

The best favor that you can do for your mental health is to learn to prioritize your level of concern, regarding a matter; thereby, you will not become overly attached to an outcome, be it good or bad.

$$\Sigma$$

Beware of hypocrites who are in total self-denial; for, they are inadvertently apt to expose their shortcomings, by that which they would so fervently condemn.

$$\Sigma$$

Never assume or be convinced that someone is psychologically free; especially, if they endeavor to slave for others' agendas and opinions.

$$\Sigma$$

Never expect a system of so-called justice to function competently; especially, if it performs its societal duties based upon the precariousness of an insatiable ego.

Once you recognize that you are a free spirit of true will, be mindful of those who would attempt to diminish your personal potential, by trying to insidiously recruit you into their conventional ways of limited thinking.

As I have personally evolved, I have learned that forgiveness can be quite empowering; but, it should not enable repeat behavior; by naively choosing to forget that which others have done.

If someone would attempt to trash your personal image; then you can reasonably assume that you have ruined the facade of that which they pretend to be.

If others were to ask, "How do we know that you are genuine?" My answer would be: "I live only to impress myself; by ever striving to become a better version of me."

Σ

Never gauge beauty, by the sole sensation of the eyes; lest, you find yourself utterly deceived by a facade of no substance.

Σ

Never assume that the nobility of a professed title will offer you immunity from the self-destructive potentials of utter greed.

Σ

Do not assume that someone cares; simply because they are good at hiding their narcissistic tendencies.

Σ

You are never wasting your time; when you firmly decide to remove yourself from the dogmatic schedule of others' expectations.

True greatness does not hinge on being a passenger of others' fickle sense of approval; it is personally driven by those who will not take a backseat, in order to avoid trying to conveniently fit in.

You can always tell the fragility of a bruised ego; because, it will go to great lengths to utterly deny its obvious vulnerabilities.

Until one is prudently ready to disavow a given sense of status, one will always remain an exhausted victim of personally having to try to prove something to others.

Choosing to be a psychological shapeshifter affords me the profound privilege of not having to prove or be concerned with telling others who or what I am; for I confidently know that by the destined winds of fate, they will eventually find out.

As long as the right-hand path of religious ideology will set perfection to be either an impractical monopoly or something that is completely unattainable, I will humbly choose to exhibit perfection; within the reasonable bounds of a prudently diabolical disposition.

$$\Sigma$$

Weak minds are always looking or hoping for others to break; for they have psychologically disabled their sense of positive resolve, by imprudently falling within the bitter cracks of personal instability.

$$\Sigma$$

As it relates to civilizations, there can be no sustained advancement of higher ideals; under the hypocritical ethics of noble savages who ignorantly assume that they are just.

$$\Sigma$$

The profound ability to tolerate others' cruelty gave me the remarkable strength of long-suffering; but, when the existential wheel turned in my favor, justice awarded me with an untold sense of delight, which was long overdue.

$$\Sigma$$

Choosing not to embrace the wisdom of eternity, humanity hastily lives as frightened misers of seeking only to accrue immediate gratification; thereby, they remain utterly convinced that they are but helpless captives of time-itself.

Jealous minds are always under the spell or the whims of those who they wish that they could be.

The last laugh will always be given to those who do not mind being taken as a joke; for, within themselves, they house the collateral potential that is prudently capable of exposing others' lack of well-being.

I find that it is okay to share wisdom's intimate secrets; for, most of them are so obvious that many would completely ignore them, by choosing to have a close-minded perspective of total disregard.

Psychic vampires are always seeking to opportunistically feed off of that which they are not willing to develop within themselves.

Depression is a very real thing; as long as you exhaustively invest your interest and time to uphold social structures and religious ideologies that are utterly lacking.

When truth speaks, it has an overwhelming presence that demands an audience of both sinners and saints alike.

It has been said that the greatest trick that the devil ever pulled was convincing the world that he didn't exist. But, I beg to differ; for with all the racial strife that humanity has propagated against each other, how could they helplessly be convinced to do the bidding of a supposedly solid red figure with two horns.

Unfortunately, I find that certain men feel that they have to occasionally invest in more weapons than is necessary; so that they will be ever reminded of their so-called sense of masculinity.

The last stand of those who realize that they are totally incompetent is typically the proxy behavior of hiding their agendas behind the unassuming minds of those who feel that they have earned total social acceptance.

For the mind that seeks comfort, the path of darkness is quite convenient; because, its ultimate psychological requirement is that you always remain loyal, by never asking the radiant question of why.

For the unevolved, blind redundancy is an established way of life; but, in an effort to experience something new, they are always seeking to recruit others, with frail hopes of liven up their dismal reality.

A mind, which has been manipulatively colonized by a religious outlook, may view DIVINITY as something that is only exclusive to those who have successfully repressed its reality.

Being free-spirited, enables the profound privilege of not having to be psychologically bound by that which others choose to deny, lie or totally refuse to accept as a possibility.

One should develop an honest sense of transparency that is so formidable that character assassins become utterly daunted; by that which someone has insidiously tasked them to do.

Amusingly, I personally do not believe in having enemies; so to somewhat avoid this unfortunate potential, I prudently choose to keep most relationships at a distance, by not elevating them pass the status of a mere acquaintance.

You can only experience psychological hurt or disappointment by others, if you allow yourself to give their opinions an advantage of esteem or significance; which, in turn, could ruin your sense of personal pride.

Delusion is very pronounced within those who try to establish control by means of deception.

Spiritual/Existential Metaphysics

Existential Musings:

WITHIN THE SINGULARITY,   EDWARD L. HANNON

ENERGY'S CONTRADISTINCTIVE SYSTEMS OF KINETIC PATTERNING
FACILITATES THE DISSASSOCIATIVE SENSE OF SPACE/TIME POTENTIALITY.

LIGHT PATTERNS FORM'S POTENTIALITIES, THROUGH
THE CATEGORICAL QUALITIES OF KINETIC ELEMENTS BEHAVING
AND THEN MOVING IN A SPECIFIED FASHION; WHICH
CONTRADISTINCTIVELY COAGULATES INTO AN EXISTENTIAL
SENSE OF SOLIDIFICATION.

BENDING A SPACE/TIME CONTINUUM BY
HYPER-DIMENSIONALLY RESHAPING THE DYNAMICS OF
A GALACTIC BUBBLE.

A QUANTUM BYPASS (WORM HOLE) IS A FREQUENCY
PORTAL; WHICH HAS A TRAJECTORY THAT CAN CIRCUMNAVIGATE
THE PROJECTED DYNAMICS OF LINEARITY.

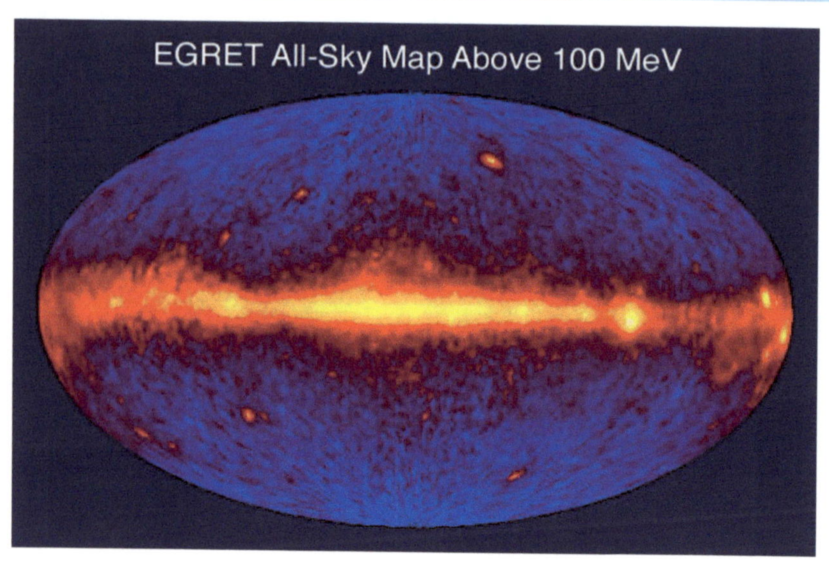

Existential Musings:

LIGHT IS THOUGHT TECHNOLOGY.

THOUGHT'S FREQUENCY IS PERVASIVE; THUS DEPENDING ON ITS MAGNITUDE, IT IS CAPABLE OF INFILTRATING OR OVERRIDING OTHER TEMPORAL FREQUENCIES.

THOUGHT'S FREQUENCY GALVANIZES AND PRE-ARRANGES EXISTENTIAL POTENTIALITY; IN ORDER TO HYPER-DYNAMICALLY FACILITATE EXPERIENTIAL POSSIBILITIES.

LOWER FREQUENCY THOUGHT, WITHIN THREE DIMENSIONAL FORM, HAS A KINETIC ENERGY-RESONANCE THAT IS HYPER-DYNAMICALLY TEMPERED BY A GRAVITATIONAL FORCE FIELD.

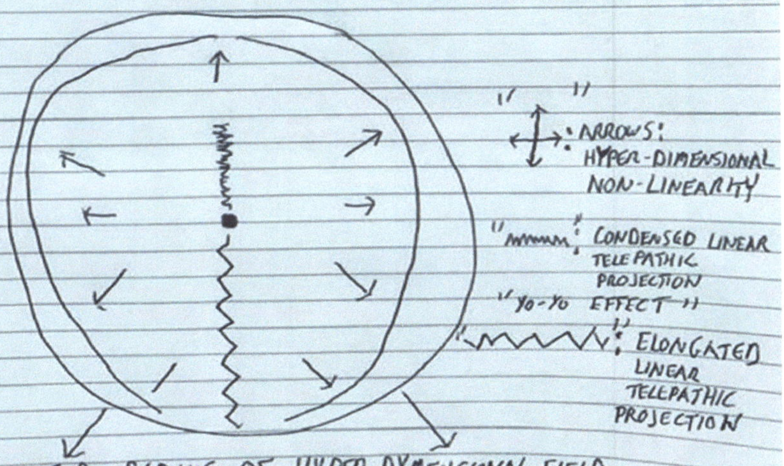

↕↔ : ARROWS: HYPER-DIMENSIONAL NON-LINEARITY

〰 : CONDENSED LINEAR TELEPATHIC PROJECTION "YO-YO EFFECT"

〰〰 : ELONGATED LINEAR TELEPATHIC PROJECTION

PROJECTED RADIUS OF HYPER-DYMENSIONAL FIELD DYNAMICS

EDWARD L. HANNON

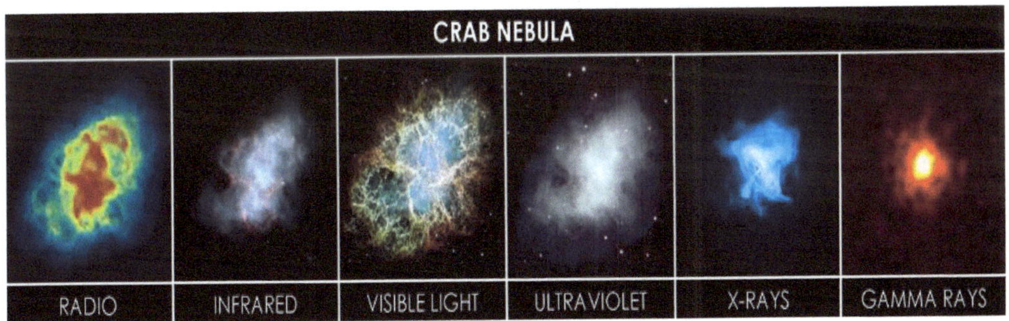

Existential Musings:

EDWARD L. HANNON

WITHIN THE SINGULARITY, SOME KINETIC PATTERN DYNAMICS AS SO INTRICATELY INTERTWINED IN THEIR DESIGN THAT THEY FACILITATE SEALANT POTENTIALITIES FOR FURTHER EXISTENTIAL POSSIBILITIES.

IT CAN BE SAID THAT COSMIC AND GAMMA RADIAL IMPRESSIONS ARE ENHANCED; ONCE, THE TYPICAL OCULAR FACULTIES HAVE KINETICALLY WITHDREW AND SHIFTED INTO MORE HYPER-RESONANT FREQUENCIES, WITHIN THE RHYTHMIC BOUNDS OF BIO-METRICAL POTENTIALITY.

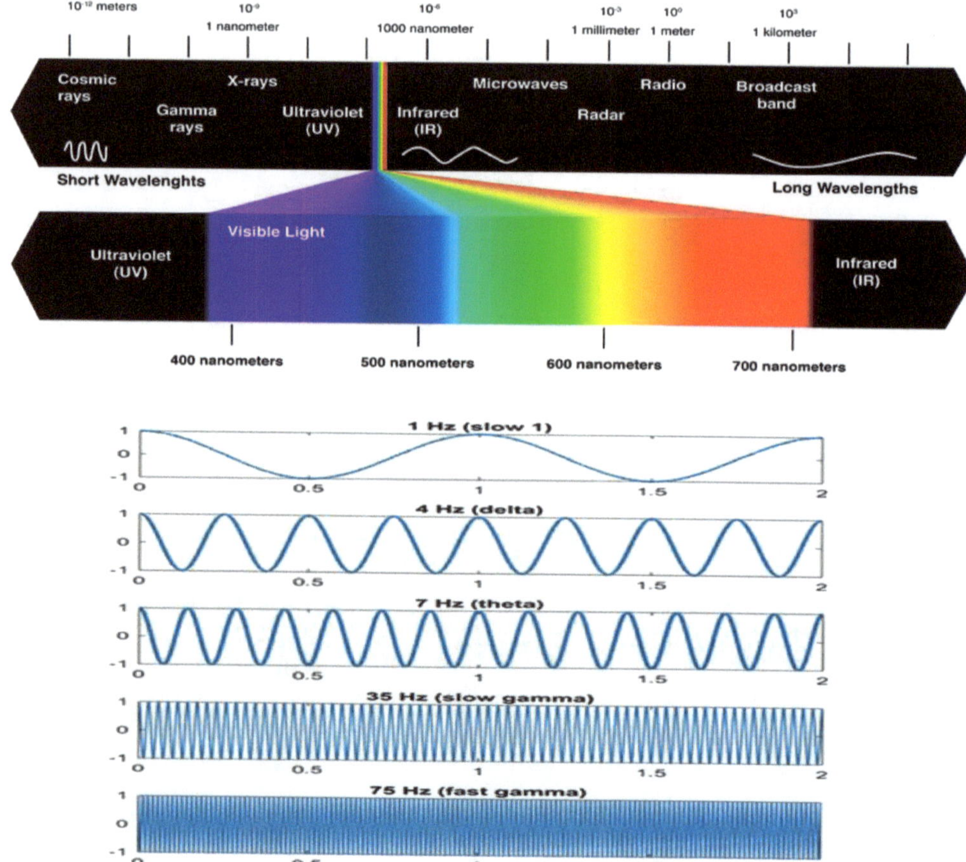

Dark Humor

Amusingly, I have met many nefarious people that would manipulatively encourage me to be the bigger person by turning the other cheek; but, I chose to be diabolically larger, by being unapologetically willing to show my complete ass.

Amusingly, you can tell that you have reached a very mature state of mental detachment; if you find yourself doom scrolling (a morbid habit of scanning media platforms for unfortunate events), but remain psychologically unbothered by what is emotively portrayed.

Humorously, I have learned to personally rejoice when others choose to unwisely listen; for it excuses me from having to display any formalities of being concerned.

Humorously, those who feel that they have much to lose, are typically the ones with the most to prove.

Amusingly, if someone were to ask, "Are you a light-worker?" My answer would be: yes; but, I am the type of light-worker who candidly exposes the darkness of that which others so desperately try to hide.

Amusingly, when you are living your truth, many may waste their time hoping that someday you will live up to their selfish expectations.

Amusingly, when you are in tune with Cosmic Order, some may perceive, condemn or denounce you to be a witch; by which, you should realize that, in spite of technological progress, humanity still has not advanced beyond the paranoia of primitive superstitions.

Humorously, you can always gauge the sexual insecurities of those who display themselves to be hyper feminine or masculine; for, their lack of confidence in their personal identity causes them to radically impose their views on how others should live their lives, and also how others should behave in the bedroom.

Humorously, self-denial can foster a deceptive tendency; which may cause someone to personally assume that they are being somehow convincing.

Amusingly, I started to no longer become a victim of self-denial; once, I prudently stopped giving a damn about what others may think of me.

Humorously, the reason, why I have become content with not growing up, is because I have not witnessed an adequate standard of maturity within adults that would give me the inspiration to do so.

Amusingly, catastrophe has no bearing on foolish minds that are hellbent on self-destruction; which is why, it may be best to channel your outrage or concern towards the exorbitant amount that it takes for their personal interment.

Amusingly, some may feel as though I will always be the same old a—hole; as though they somehow expected me to receive an anatomical transplant of another.

Humorously, if others are prone to not take you seriously, do not be offended; because typically they are desperately trying to defend their egotistical state of total BS.

Humorously, this picture is symbolic of my enthusiasm; when witnessing the personal turmoil of those who are prone to scoff at sound advice.

Afterthought

My Collective Works:

Immortal Tomorrow

The Acquisitions of the Spirit: The Rise of Vibrational Consciousness

The Consciousness of the Spirit: Philosychology: Edisms and Edimous Concepts

The Path and Pinnacle of Consciousness

The Reinforcement of Consciousness

There is Nothing, but the Fractal Nature of GOD

To Serve and Protect

"Day by Day" Oracle Book Reading: "First Pick a Number! (1-31)"

From Nothing

Mystic Consciousness

Nothing More to be Said

Quantum Discourses about the Reality of Energy

Sapient Awakening: The Rise of HOMO-DEUS

Sapient State: The HOMO-DEUS Consciousness Realized

Sapient Tomorrow: Risen Angels and Respectful Demons

Sentient Being

Sentient Comprehension

Sentient Reasoning: A Small Book of Occult Revelations and Mysticism

Sentient Understanding: Mastering One's Demons

Thank You, Chaplain: For The Uncomfortable Truth

The Comedy of DIVINE Madness

Always remember that within a twenty-four hour span of a day, sixteen hours are typically devoted to being fixed within a third-dimensional continuum of space/time possibility; whereas, the other eight hours house the existential boundlessness of multi-dimensional potentiality.

Being a psychological shapeshifter enables me the uncanny ability to peer into the souls of those that feign sincerity; under the false pretenses of a noble identity.

The profound reason, why the ancients only kept a cosmic calendar for only about seven thousand years or so, was because they ultimately knew that it would be subject to eventually expire; due to periodic shifts in earth's orbital position, which may drastically result in the way that the architecture of time can be perceived and also calculated.